How Not to be the Perfect

Celeb

This is a STAR FIRE book

STAR FIRE
Crabtree Hall, Crabtree Lane
Fulham, London SW6 6TY
United Kingdom

www.star-fire.co.uk

First published 2007

07 09 11 10 08

1 3 5 7 9 10 8 6 4 2

Star Fire is part of The Foundry Creative Media Company Limited

The CIP record for this book is available from the British Library.

ISBN: 978 1 84451 942 2

Printed in China

Thanks to: Cat Emslie, Andy Frostick, Victoria Lyle,
Sara Robson, Nick Wells

How Not to be the Perfect

Celeb

Ulysses Brave

STAR FIRE

Foreword

There are so many rules today, scrupulously compiled by faceless committees of governing and busy bodies. Over the years many people have appealed to me for clarity and purpose on such matters. They say that it is difficult to know how to behave in modern society, so I have penned some careful advice based on simple, old-fashioned common sense.

Ulysses Brave

In the right circles,
facial hair can be
most attractive.

Whatever you are doing — shopping, partying, travelling, gossiping — always keep your eyes sharp for the best fame-enhancing opportunity.

*Don't despair if the latest
anti-ageing treatments
take their time to work.*

Don't get too close to the
paparazzi's zoom lenses, they will
reveal all the little blemishes
and pimples you've taken
so much care to hide.

Try not to wear sunglasses for too long in the full sun, otherwise tell-tale rings will develop just as you get ready for the Hello! mag shoot.

In breaks between fashion shoots, stock up on some tasty, organic foods.

Botox has helped thousands of aspiring celebrities to achieve beauty. But beware, there are the occasional side effects.

Rubbing shoulders with ageing rock stars can be an overwhelming experience.

Fake tan looks good all year round, so there's no need for inconvenient weekend breaks with the general public.

*All the best celebs have
a skill or profession to
fall back on.*

The difference between a
D-list and a C-list celeb
is not intelligence but
opportunistic cuteness.

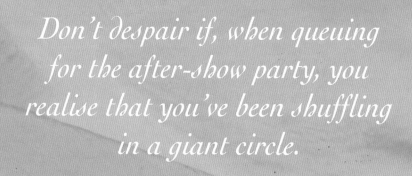

Don't despair if, when queuing for the after-show party, you realise that you've been shuffling in a giant circle.

Of course, if you're in a queue in the first place you need to rethink your celeb strategy.

High heels are the celeb's best friend, especially when trying to peek into the local WAGs' dinner do.

When trying to crash a top party, put on your best make-up and smile your way past the bouncers.

*Even close-up, the true
celeb has perfect skin.*

Publicity shy celebs will not increase their celeb status. Pretend to hide, but always make sure you know when your picture is being taken.

Cheek and lip control
form an essential part of
the celeb's appeal.

Always look your best for the cameras. A great shot in the glossy mags will always raise your celebrity profile.

Size zero fashions won't necessarily suit the body shape of every celeb.

Consider commissioning a trendy out-of-focus publicity shot if your celebrity status is not derived from your fabulous looks.

There is a subtle hierarchy in the WAG and D-list celeb community. You too can aspire to marry a cousin who once went out with a TV soap star.

Wake up every morning and exclaim, "I am gorgeous! I am successful!"

Always wear the latest
catwalk fashions.

How to be a Celeb,
Rule no. 17:
Remove all facial hair before
an important party.

Partying all night can make you grumpy and unattractive to those all-important TV talent scouts.

Your complexion will thank you if you always carry a handy bottle of mineral water with you.

Waiting for a taxi early in the morning, after an exotic after-show reality TV party, can be hard on the legs.

*Don't be embarrassed by
your fanatical need for
an all-over tan.*

Mastication in public is acceptable but only in full eye make-up.

Bodyguards are an unfortunate necessity. Be kind to them.

When meeting other celebs, make sure you show your best side.

Try to avoid getting drunk
in public – it will only get
in the papers.

If you want to scratch out your nearest rival's eyes, wait until they are asleep after a long binge drinking session.

Come back soon!